DUBAI
A COLOUR-CODED GUIDE TO THE HOT 'HOODS

MARINA
This vertical neighbourhood is the cultural and leisure counterweight to Sheikh Zayed

SHEIKH ZAYED
Dubai's glittering-glass business district also boasts many fine-dining and nightlife venues

DOWNTOWN
The home of the tallest building in the world is fast becoming the heart of the city

DEIRA
Chaotic and crumbling, the old town provides a rare but charming taste of the Middle East

AL QUOZ
Art galleries and ateliers now occupy the warehouses of Dubai's gritty industrial zone

BUR DUBAI
This 1960s suburb is a hotchpotch of heritage architecture and great Indian restaurants

beachside playground

two golf clubs and a park

For a full description of each neighbourhood, see the introduction.
Featured venues are colour-coded, according to the district in which they are located.

GW01561491

PHOTOGRAPHERS

Nagib Khazaka
Dubai city view, inside
front cover
Dubai Marina, pp010-011
Jumeirah Emirates
Towers, p012
InterContinental Festival
City, p020, p021
Al Ahmadiya, p034, p035
Mojo Gallery, pp036-037
Pierchic, p038, p039
The Edge, p041
Reflets, p047
The One Deli, pp048-049
Rare Restaurant, p051
The Roof Top, pp052-053
Okku, pp054-055
Left Bank, p057
Zuma, pp058-059
Nadine Knotzer, p063
Burj Khalifa, p065
The Gate, pp066-067
O-14 Building, p069
O' de Rose, p073
Villa Moda, pp076-077
Shiffa, p079
Meydan Racecourse,
pp084-085

Raymond Meier
Imam Mosque, p096;
Friday Mosque, p097,
Isfahan

Roger Moukarzel
Almaz by
Momo, p050

Mai Nordahn
Clock Tower Roundabout,
pp014-015
XVA, p029
Zaatar w Zeit, p033
The Lime Tree Café, p046
Indego, p056
National Bank of
Dubai, p068
Dubai Creek Golf & Yacht
Club, pp070-071
Amara, p081
Ski Dubai, pp086-087

Jonathan de Villiers
Burj Al Arab, p013

WALLPAPER* CITY GUIDES

Editorial Director
Richard Cook

Art Director
Loran Stosskopf
Editor
Rachael Moloney
Author
Warren Singh-Bartlett
Deputy Editor
Jeremy Case
Managing Editor
Jessica Diamond

Designer
Lara Collins

Map Illustrator
Russell Bell

Photography Editor
Sophie Corben
Photography Assistant
Robin Key

Sub-Editors
Vanessa Harriss
Vicky McGinlay
Editorial Assistant
Ella Marshall

Interns
Ayse Koklu
Kerry Norwood

**Wallpaper* Group
Editor-in-Chief**
Tony Chambers
Publishing Director
Gord Ray

Contributors
Jana Khoury
Daisy Ellen Omissi

Wallpaper* ® is a
registered trademark
of IPC Media Limited

First published 2007
Second edition (revised
and updated) 2011
© 2007 and 2011
IPC Media Limited

ISBN 978 0 7148 6089 3

PHAIDON

Phaidon Press Limited
Regent's Wharf
All Saints Street
London N1 9PA

Phaidon Press Inc
180 Varick Street
New York, NY 10014

Phaidon® is a registered
trademark of Phaidon
Press Limited

www.phaidon.com

A CIP Catalogue record for
this book is available from
the British Library.

All prices are correct at
time of going to press,
but are subject to change.

Printed in China

Shangri-La Hotel 026

Room rates:
double, DH1,200;
Horizon Club, DH1,600;
Presidential Suite, DH14,000
Sheikh Zayed Road
Al Satwa side
T 343 8888
www.shangri-la.com

XVA 029

Room rates:
double, from DH350
Al Fahidi roundabout
Behind Basta Art Café
T 353 5383
www.xvahotel.com

Yas Hotel 092

Room rates:
double, from DH430
Yas Marina
Abu Dhabi
T 02 656 0000
www.theyashotel.com

Six Senses Hideaway Zighy Bay 098

Room rates:
double, from DH3,880
Zighy Bay
Musandam Peninsula
Oman
T 00 968 2673 5555
www.sixsenses.com

HOTELS

ADDRESSES AND ROOM RATES

The Address Downtown 024
Room rates:
double, from DH1,200;
Deluxe Room, from DH1,200;
Premier Fountain View, from DH1,600;
Spa Suite, from DH3,600
Emaar Boulevard
T 436 8888
www.theaddress.com

Armani Hotel 017
Room rates:
double, from DH3,120
1 Emaar Boulevard
T 888 3888
dubai.armanihotels.com

Atlantis 016
Room rates:
double, DH3,100
The Palm
Crescent Road
T 426 2000
www.atlantisthepalm.com

Banyan Tree Al Wadi 102
Room rates:
double, from DH2,350
Al Mazraa
Ras Al Khaimah
T 07 206 7777
www.banyantree.com

Desert Palm Retreat 030
Room rates:
double, from DH1,250;
Palm Suite, from DH1,250
Al Awir Road
T 323 8888
desertpalm.peraquum.com

Grosvenor House 028
Room rates:
double, from DH900
West Marina Beach
T 399 8888
www.grosvenorhouse-dubai.com

InterContinental Festival City 020
Room rates:
double, from DH1,500;
Presidential Suite, from DH7,500
Dubai Festival City
T 701 1111
www.ichotelsgroup.com/intercontinental

The Jumeirah Garden Guesthouse 016
Room rates:
double, from DH450
Villa 76
Street 14a
Al Manara
T 956 2854

Park Hyatt 022
Room rates:
double, from DH1,530;
Royal Suite, from DH19,530
Dubai Creek Golf & Yacht Club
Al Garhoud Road
T 602 1234
www.dubai.park.hyatt.com

Qasr Al Sarab Desert Resort 094
Room rates:
double, from DH2,440
1 Qasr Al Sarab Road
Abu Dhabi
T 02 886 2088
www.qasralsarab.anantara.com

RESOURCES

CITY GUIDE DIRECTORY

A

Al Ahmadiya 034
Al Khor Street
T 226 0286
www.dubaitourism.ae/cultureheritage

Almaz by Momo 050
3rd floor
Harvey Nichols
Mall of the Emirates
Sheikh Zayed Road
T 409 8877
www.altayer.com

Amara 081
Park Hyatt
Dubai Creek Golf & Yacht Club
Al Garhoud Road
T 602 1234
www.dubai.park.hyatt.com

B

Al Beit Al Baghdadi 040
Al Muteena Street
T 273 7064

Belgian Beer Café 051
Crowne Plaza Hotel
Dubai Festival City
T 701 2267
www.ichotelsgroup.com

Blue Souk 100
Corniche Street
Sharjah

Boom & Mellow 078
Shop F47
1st floor
Mall of the Emirates
Sheikh Zayed Road
T 341 3993
www.boomandmellow.com

Al Boom Diving 080
Al Wasl Road
T 342 2993
www.alboomdiving.com

Burj Al Arab 013
Jumeirah Beach Road
T 301 7777
www.burj-al-arab.com

Burj Khalifa 065
1 Emaar Boulevard
T 888 8124
www.burjkhalifa.ae

C

**Caramel Restaurant
& Lounge** 042
Level 2
Gate Village
Building 3
DIFC
T 425 6677
www.carameldubai.com

Carbon 12 062
Warehouse D37
Street 8
Al Serkal Avenue
Al Quoz 1
T 050 464 4392
www.carbon12dubai.com

Clock Tower Roundabout 014
Al Maktoum Road/Umm Hurair Road

D

Desert Safari Dubai 088
T 357 2200
www.desertsafaridubai.com

Dream Girl 072
Al Fahidi Street
Next to Meena Bazaar
T 352 6463

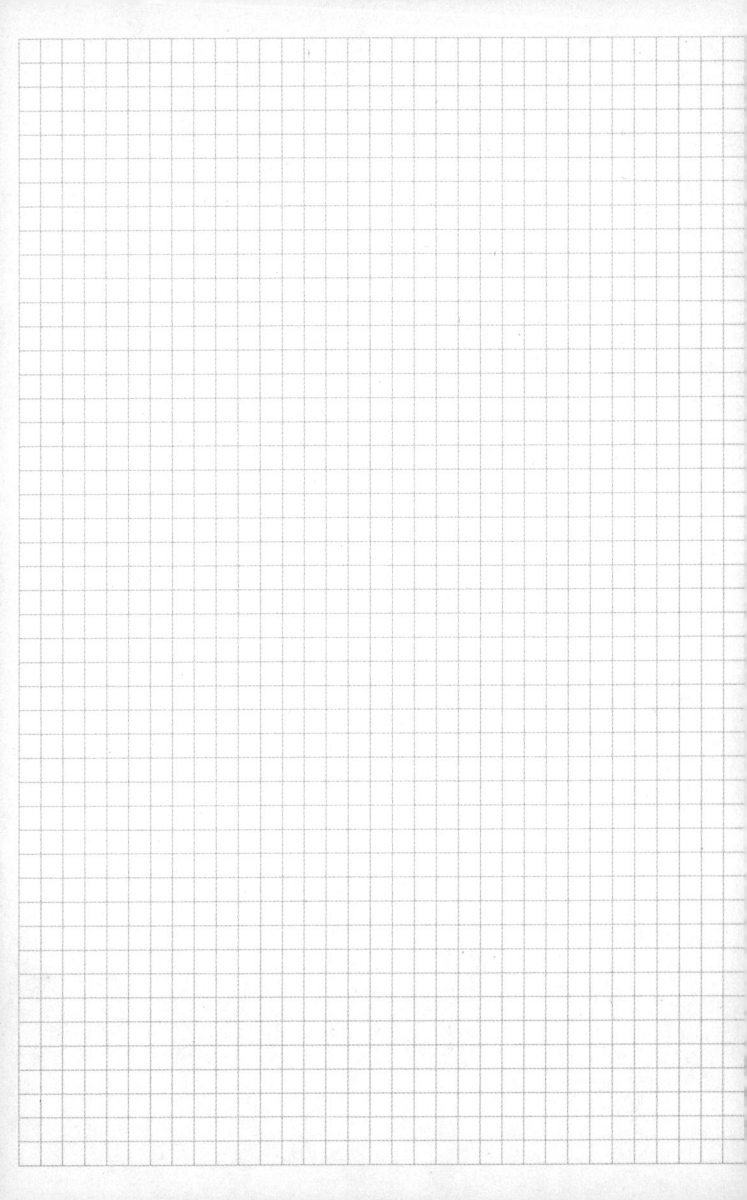

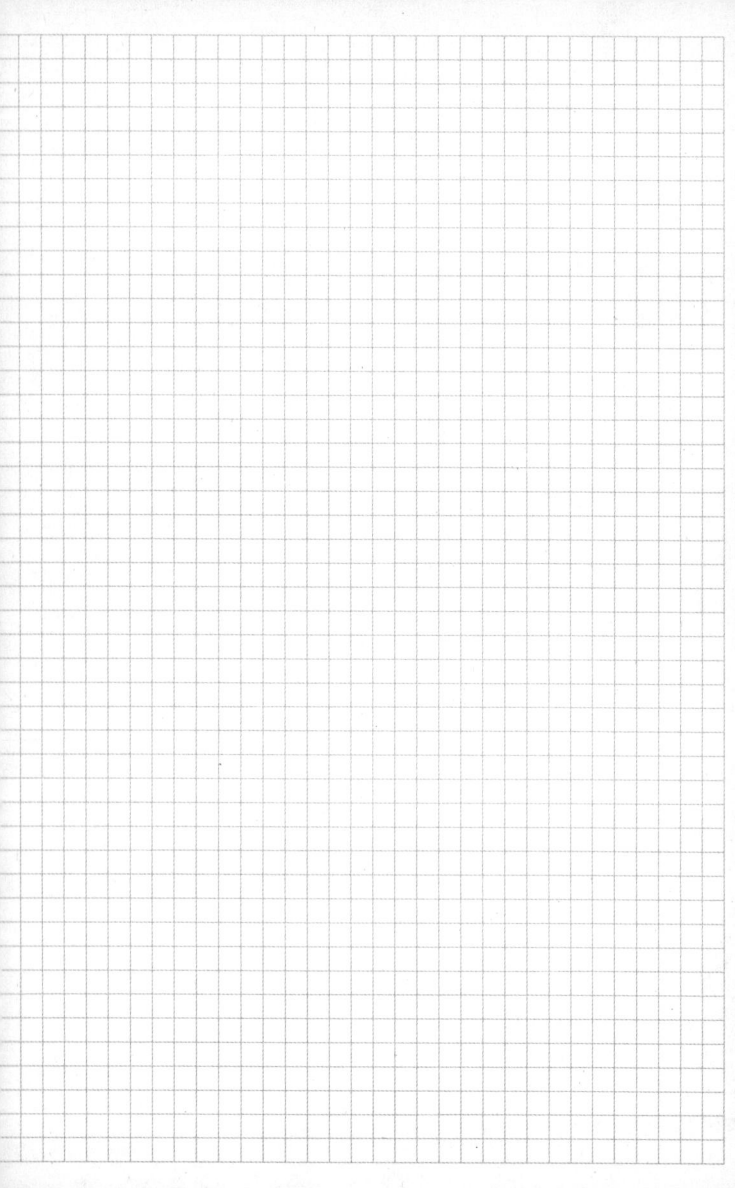

NOTES
SKETCHES AND MEMOS

DUBAI
THE CITY AT A GLANCE

Business Bay
Sadly, of the 200 or so waterfront towers that
will comprise the city's new corporate heart,
only Reiser + Umemoto's 'Swiss cheese' 0-14
Building (see p069) is likely to be memorable.

Dubai Metro
The metro is a model of efficiency, although
not that practical as many stations are located
far from the places you'll probably want to visit.

Burj Khalifa
Sometimes bigger really is better. The world's
highest tower is one of the most beautiful pieces
of architecture in the city.
See p065

The Index
Lord Foster's massive slab of a building is the
elegant antithesis of the gaudy glass ziggurats
lining Sheikh Zayed Road.
See p064

The Address Downtown
Lit in brilliant strips of blue and white by night,
The Address hotel complex has a slew of great
restaurants and the best pool area in town.
See p024

Jumeirah Emirates Towers
These were the tallest structures in Dubai for
nine years and are still a beloved landmark.
See p012

Bur Dubai
A mix of the old and the new, the Bur Dubai
district is home to excellent Indian restaurants,
glitzy malls, Al Fahidi Fort and the restored
merchant homes and palaces of Bastakiya.

INTRODUCTION

THE CHANGING FACE OF THE URBAN SCENE

Under its Middle Eastern veneer, Dubai is really Asian. Arabic is the national language and Islam the official religion, but while you'll hear a '*salaam aleikum*' or two, Arabic is notable only for its absence. As are the Arabs. Emiratis account for around 10 per cent of the population, South Asians for more than half.

Dubai embraces contradiction. A Gulf state with little oil of its own, it is an economic powerhouse. Poised between the hard-line Islamic republics of Saudi Arabia and Iran, it is open and fairly tolerant. The city also has global clout, though its population is barely 1.8 million. The speed of development may have slowed, but Dubai hasn't given up on its vaulting ambitions. The plan to increase the population to five million and tourist arrivals to 15 million by 2010 did not succeed, and talk is now of achieving these goals by 2015 instead. Impossible? Maybe, but that's a word still rarely used in the city modesty did not build.

Perhaps it's the squeaky clean urban environment. Perhaps it's the good life. Either way, people keep coming. *Stepford Wives*-perfect, Dubai feels like a giant resort, at least the parts that don't look like a building site. Whether you see it as a global hub or a giant transit lounge, the city is a modern phenomenon that tempers its bad habits (it's unsustainable and fractured along class and racial lines) with a fervent belief that everything can and should be changed. That alone makes it a marvel.

ESSENTIAL INFO
FACTS, FIGURES AND USEFUL ADDRESSES

TOURIST OFFICE
Visitor Information Bureau
Deira City Centre
T 294 8615
www.dubaitourism.ae

TRANSPORT
Car hire
Avis
T 224 5219
Hertz
T 224 5222
Public transport
www.rta.ae
The metro runs 6am-11pm, Saturday to
Thursday, and 2pm-midnight on Friday
Taxis
Dubai Taxi
T 208 0808
There are also taxi ranks outside shopping
malls and the larger hotels

EMERGENCY SERVICES
Ambulance/Police
T 999
Fire
T 997
24-hour pharmacy
Binsina Pharmacy
Al Rigga Road
T 224 7650

EMBASSIES/CONSULATES
British Embassy
Al Seef Road
T 309 4444
www.ukinuae.fco.gov.uk
US Consulate-General
Dubai World Trade Centre
Sheikh Zayed Road
T 311 6000
dubai.usconsulate.gov

MONEY
American Express
2nd floor
Hermitage Building
Zabeel Road
T 336 5000
www.americanexpress.com

POSTAL SERVICES
Post office
Abu Hail Road
T 262 2222
Shipping
UPS
T 339 1939
www.ups.com

BOOKS
**The Architecture of the United Arab
Emirates** by Salma Samar Damluji
(Garnet Publishing)
Dubai Architecture & Design
edited by Sabina Marreiros (Daab)

WEBSITES
Art
www.thethirdline.com
Newspaper
www.thenational.ae

COST OF LIVING
**Taxi from Dubai International Airport
to Sheikh Zayed Road**
45 dirhams
Cappuccino
16 dirhams
Packet of cigarettes
7.50 dirhams
Daily newspaper
3 dirhams
Bottle of champagne
1,200 dirhams

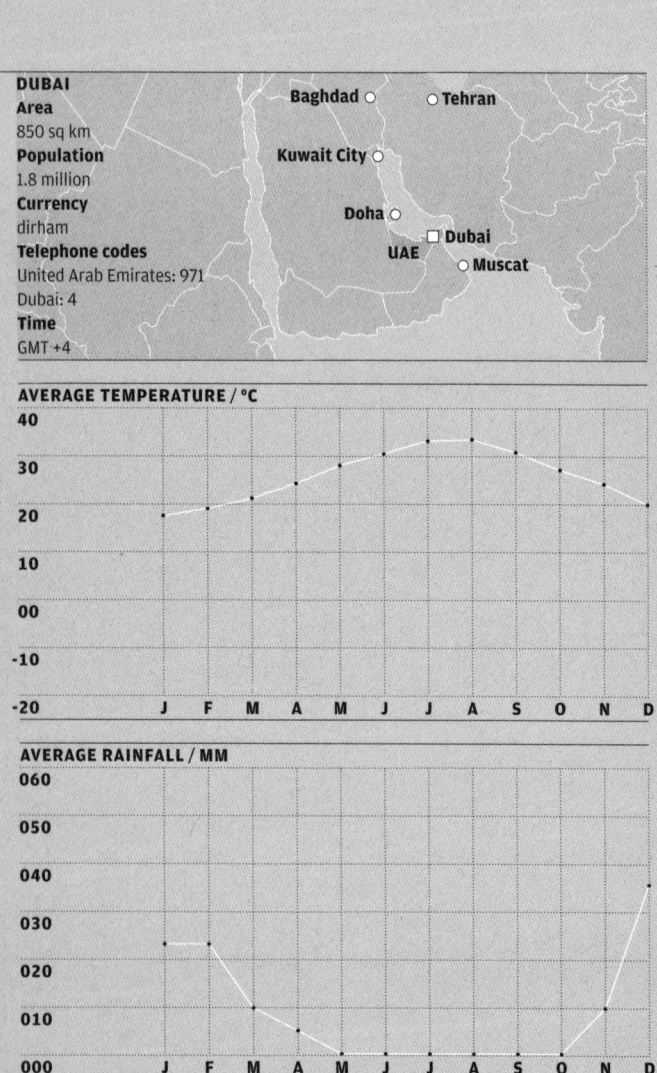

DUBAI
Area
850 sq km
Population
1.8 million
Currency
dirham
Telephone codes
United Arab Emirates: 971
Dubai: 4
Time
GMT +4

Baghdad ○   ○ Tehran

Kuwait City ○

Doha ○
□ Dubai
UAE   ○ Muscat

AVERAGE TEMPERATURE / °C

40											
30											
20											
10											
00											
-10											
-20	J	F	M	A	M	J	J	A	S	O	N	D

AVERAGE RAINFALL / MM

060											
050											
040											
030											
020											
010											
000	J	F	M	A	M	J	J	A	S	O	N	D

NEIGHBOURHOODS

THE AREAS YOU NEED TO KNOW AND WHY

To help you navigate the city, we've chosen the most interesting districts (see the map inside the back cover) and underlined featured venues in colour, according to their location (see below); those venues that are outside these areas are not coloured.

MARINA

Located between Sheikh Zayed Road's shopping meccas Ibn Battuta (T 362 1900) and Mall of the Emirates (T 409 9000), and encompassing the swish Emirates Hills and Palm areas, the very vertical Marina is one of Dubai's newest districts. It's the stomping ground of the creatives from nearby Internet and Media Cities.

SHEIKH ZAYED

This glittering strip of glass towers may not be visible from space, but it certainly dominates the city skyline. Spotless and business-oriented, the central artery is everything brave new Dubai wants to be. Its refined restaurants and nightlife draw expense-account visitors and expats.

DOWNTOWN

On its way to becoming the heart of the city, this is one of the few areas to attract people from its southern and northern fringes. The focus of their interest is the astonishing Burj Khalifa (see p065) and the faux historicism of Old Town, plus eateries such as The Edge (see p041).

DEIRA

Cramped, chaotic and crumbling, Deira could not be less like shiny new Dubai if it tried. This pedestrian paradise finally gives visitors a sense of being in the Middle East. Wander around the souks, visit the city's first school (see p034) or take a ride on one of the water taxis plying the Creek.

AL QUOZ

A dusty, industrial neighbourhood where the bulk of Dubai's manufacturing is done, Al Quoz has become the centre of the city's burgeoning creative scene, and includes a number of printing and film-production companies. Many of its warehouses have been transformed into art galleries, such as Mojo (see p036), and artists' ateliers.

BUR DUBAI

The child of Dubai's 1960s building boom looks a little rough around the edges, but it is home to great Indian eateries and a hefty chunk of the city's architectural heritage. Big draws are Al Fahidi Fort, the Bastakia area and restored but no longer inhabited royal residences in Shindagha.

JUMEIRAH

The low-rise mix of villas, cafés and malls lends Dubai's premier beachfront district a more relaxed air than the rest of the city. Eat at The Lime Tree Café (see p046), chill on the pristine public beach and explore the side streets hiding boutiques and spas, all aimed at Dubai's deeper pockets.

CREEK

As the Creek winds towards the wildlife sanctuary of Khor Dubai, it turns from busy waterway to urban leisure space. The ongoing Festival City development will add bars and clubs to the restaurants, such as Reflets (see p047), lining the river near the Golf & Yacht Club (see p070).

LANDMARKS

THE SHAPE OF THE CITY SKYLINE

For a city that has made its reputation on superlatives – the tallest tower, the most luxurious hotel – you'd expect Dubai to be awash with impressive buildings. But in reality, when it comes to finding structures that deserve to be called landmarks, that overgrown flagpole in Jumeirah aside, pickings are slim. At least for now.

Blame this on Dubai's twin weaknesses: its relative youth and a development plan that has always placed making money before building anything memorable. As a consequence, city planners tore down almost everything historical years ago. Of course, there are always the two towers – the sparkling Burj Khalifa (see p065) and its little sister, the Burj Al Arab (see p013) – but after a while, you'll suspect the latter's inescapable presence on T-shirts and postcards, and its transformation into stuffed toys, incense burners and gold-plated paperweights, proves that Dubai's most recognisable symbol is pretty much its only recognisable symbol.

Perhaps it is best to consider the landmark question on the macro, not the micro, level. From its beginnings as a speck on the map – a former pearl-trading town where less-interesting airlines stopped to refuel – Dubai has grown into a sprawling, rapidly metastasising city that, shades of Ozymandias aside, sees itself not just as a global hub but as *the* global hub. Forget individual buildings, Dubai's most impressive landmark may just be itself. *For full addresses, see Resources.*

Dubai Marina

This is one of the largest manmade marinas on the planet. Of course. For now, the 40 towers of neighbouring Jumeirah Beach Residence, which approaches a Hong Kong-esque density, constitute the largest single-phase residential development in the world, and the marina marks the southernmost extent of Dubai. On a clear day, it is visible from almost 20km away and, seen on the drive in from Abu Dhabi, it almost suggests a city wall. It certainly declares that you have arrived. As one of Dubai's most desirable locations, the marina is also home to a few of its more interesting buildings, chief of which will be Skidmore, Owings & Merrill's Infinity Tower. Once it is finished in 2011, the 307m twisting structure, which resembles a taller, sleeker version of Calatrava's Turning Torso in Malmö, will dominate the marina's northern end.
Sheikh Zayed Road

Jumeirah Emirates Towers

Near the World Trade Centre and right at the entrance to Sheikh Zayed Road, two equilateral glass-and-steel triangles rise 305m and 350m into the air. One is a hotel, the other an office building; and the two are linked by Dubai's most exclusive mall, The Boulevard. Set in 170,000 sq m of landscaping that includes a waterfall and a garden, the NORR-designed towers dominate the otherwise low-rise financial district around them. The office tower, which opened in 2000, was the city's tallest finished building for nine years. The pair have been likened to pencil sharpeners and bottle openers, but they occupy a soft spot in many locals' hearts, being among the first of Dubai's buildings to gain international attention.

Sheikh Zayed Road, T 330 0000, www.jumeirah.com

Burj Al Arab

Okay, so the WS Atkins exterior resembles a giant Teflon beetle sitting on its haunches, and the KCA International interior is so overwrought that your initial response may be laughter, but there is still something magnificent about your first sight of this hotel. Perhaps it's the way the building appears to catch the breeze when viewed from the side or perhaps it's because, at 321m, it is one of the tallest hotels in the world. Once inside, your impression may not be as charitable. At more than 180m high, the atrium is eye-popping, but 'signature experiences' like a submarine ride to the restaurant, are fairground, and the hubristic demand that you buy a coffee or souvenir just to set foot in the lobby is beyond irritating.
Jumeirah Beach Road, T 301 7777, www.burj-al-arab.com

Clock Tower Roundabout
For many years, this modest roundabout was one of Dubai's most prominent landmarks. Built in 1962, when there were barely any paved roads to speak of, its slender, curved brackets are meant to evoke classical Islamic architecture. The clock mechanism they support was a gift to Dubai's then ruler, Sheikh Rashid, from his son-in-law.
Al Maktoum Road/Umm Hurair Road

HOTELS

WHERE TO STAY AND WHICH ROOMS TO BOOK

It is unfortunate that Dubai's most famous hotel is also its most garish. Fortunately, the self-styled 'seven star' Burj Al Arab (see p013) is not representative. On the downside, Dubai doesn't really do budget accommodation, although some of the small business hotels clustered in Bur Dubai and Deira offer reasonable deals. The few genuine boutique properties, in the sense of intimate and luxe, are The Jumeirah Garden Guesthouse (Villa 76, Street 14a, Al Manara, T 956 2854), XVA (see p029) and the Desert Palm Retreat (see p030). On the plus side, competition is fierce. All the hotels offer some 'signature' product and pride themselves on the warmth of their 'traditional Arab' hospitality, even if this is dispensed by Asians. The result is that, even at the lower end of the scale, service is courteous and generally very efficient.

During peak season, seemingly any time apart from summer, finding a room is a nightmare. Hotels feature heavily in Dubai's expansion and each of its new 'cities' include a few – though, at the time of writing, some projects were on hold, including the much-hyped Hydropolis underwater hotel. The most ballyhooed additions are the Armani (opposite) and Sol Kerzner's Atlantis (Crescent Road, T 426 2000) on The Palm Jumeirah. Plans exist for a W, a second One&Only and a Trump International, while a Palazzo Versace, with a chilled-sand beach, should open in 2011. *For full addresses and room rates, see Resources.*

Armani Hotel

From the moment you enter the lobby (above) of the first Armani hotel, located on the lower eight and 38th and 39th floors of the Burj Khalifa (see p065), you are ushered into a world that has the designer's stamp all over it, from the furniture to the products in the spa. No effort is spared to make guests feel like royalty but there are some quibbles. The minimalism can be grating and, while the palette of muted earth tones comes as a relief after the gilt elsewhere in the city, it's unlikely to win over anyone not already enamoured with Armani's home-furnishings line. For the price, the standard rooms, like the Armani Classic (overleaf), are small. Wraparound balconies make the corner suites more spacious.
1 Emaar Boulevard, T 888 3888, dubai.armanihotels.com

Armani Classic Room

InterContinental Festival City

The first thing you notice about this hotel is its smiling doormen, who must stand at least 2m tall. The next is the glossy lobby with rainforest-sized floral displays and crystal-studded loungers, which are a menace to anything chiffon but which sparkle seductively in the light-filled interior. The rooms are equally polished, and the baths fill theatrically from a spout in the ceiling. Thanks to the hotel's Creek-front location, the rooms at the rear boast uninterrupted views across the water to the spires of Sheikh Zayed Road. For a taste of the high life, check in to the Presidential Suite (above and right). Clean and crisp, it's favoured by the kind of guests who prefer the anonymity of the in-room check-in, an adjacent pad for their bodyguard, and a bathroom-with-a-view that verges on a spa.
Dubai Festival City, T 701 1111,
www.ichotelsgroup.com/intercontinental

Park Hyatt

Nestled between the two halves of Dubai Creek Golf & Yacht Club (see p070), the Hyatt's whitewashed Moorish exterior, with its *zellige* tiles, sparkling blue cupolas and tropical greenery, only hints at the glamour within. The modern, airy guest rooms, some of which feature open-plan bathrooms, are pitch perfect, and the Royal Suite (above) is suitably decadent. The courtyard pool, waterfront bar, fine dining and Amara spa (see p081), with its gorgeous Tranquility Garden (left), are understated and super-elegant, and make the Hyatt a one-stop destination. *Dubai Creek Golf & Yacht Club, T 602 1234, www.dubai.park.hyatt.com*

The Address Downtown

Despite the self-important name, and the hotel's home in a tower whose design and twin antennae give it the appearance of a 306m-tall Dalek, The Address Downtown is sexy and knows it. The first of a chain scattered across the city, the hotel eschews bright and brash for low-lit and sophisticated, as in the lobby (right). It's also wired to the nines. With its online services and paperless procedures, The Address has doffed its flat cap to the media darlings and gives off a vibe that is equal parts Silicon Valley, mod Middle East and pan-Asian chic. The Deluxe Rooms are snug, while the Premier Fountain View Rooms (above) are slightly larger, though there's only a Venetian blind between the bed and the bathroom. Or plump for a Spa Suite, which has a terrace with a jacuzzi.
Emaar Boulevard, T 436 8888, www.theaddress.com

Shangri-La Hotel
Essentially, this is a business hotel, with its eyes on CEO-class patrons. Ignore the lower levels and reserve a Horizon Club room on the 40th and 41st floors or Presidential Suite (pictured). All come with capacious beds and Aigner toiletries. Service is seamless and there is a heart-warming attention to detail. *Sheikh Zayed Road, T 343 8888, www.shangri-la.com*

Grosvenor House

From the welcome drink and chilled towel that greet you on arrival in the lobby (above) to the appetisers laid out in your room, the Grosvenor prides itself on being a class act. It's located in the Marina district and, as new developments are finished, Dubai's centre of gravity will shift the hotel's way. Looking all Manhattan-in-the-1930s from the outside, its blue-neon exterior lighting belies the sophisticated Asian interior. The feel is carried through to the rooms, which are styled with dark wood and cream upholstery, creating a Zen-like ambience. The beds are big enough for a harem and rooms overlook the ever-rising Palm. *West Marina Beach, T 399 8888, www.grosvenorhouse-dubai.com*

XVA

Housed in a renovated coral-stone-and-adobe home in Bastakiya, XVA is unique. Not only does the property offer guests the chance to experience an upscale version of life in a Dubai that disappeared some 75 years ago, but the tasteful way the eight rooms have been decorated with darkwood furniture, curtained bedsteads and mother-of-pearl-inlaid furnishings by Lebanese designer Nada Debs makes them a pleasure to stay in. Also an art gallery, café and boutique, the hotel is the work of American owner and long-time Dubai resident Mona Hauser, an erudite guide to all things Emirati. The breezy rooftop terrace is a refreshing spot on hot nights, whereas the courtyard (above) is the place to relax in winter.

Al Fahidi roundabout, behind Basta Art Café, T 353 5383, www.xvahotel.com

Desert Palm Retreat
Located where the city meets the sand, this hotel/resort is set in 60 hectares of land and attracts the horsey set with stables and four polo fields. It is also a great base for desert excursions. Stay in a contemporary villa with a private garden or in the well-appointed Palm Suites (pictured). Dine at Rare (see p051). *Al Awir Road, T 323 8888, desertpalm.peraquum.com*

24 HOURS

SEE THE BEST OF THE CITY IN JUST ONE DAY

Begin your day with a piping-hot *mankoushe* at Lebanese fast-food chain Zaatar w Zeit (opposite) on Sheikh Zayed Road. Afterwards, make your way across the Creek and through the narrow streets of Deira to the beautifully restored Al Ahmadiya school (see p034) to see what traditional Gulf architecture looked like before breeze blocks, concrete and curtain walls took over. While you're in the neighbourhood, rummage around the souks (the Gold, Deira and Spice souks are within walking distance) in search of fluorescent Syrian trousers, Persian rugs and gold bullion. Then travel back across the Creek by *abra* (water taxi) and head uptown.

With lunchtime approaching, pause for a bite to eat at one of the cafés Downtown, such as More Café (Dubai Mall, T 339 8934) or the nearby Shakespeare and Co (Souk Al Bahar, T 425 7971). Suitably fortified, spend your afternoon in Al Quoz, where old factories and warehouses have been converted into ateliers and art galleries, most of them white-walled boxes with polished concrete floors and acres of space. It is hard to overestimate the importance of this neighbourhood, which has been instrumental in transforming Dubai into one of the Gulf's major art hubs.

Counter any cultural fatigue by dropping in to Pierchic (see p038), the Madinat Jumeirah's wooden château-sur-mer, for drinks and then dinner, as the sun sets over the Gulf.
For full addresses, see Resources.

08.30 Zaatar w Zeit

An outpost of Beirut in Dubai, this Lebanese chain is the perfect breakfast spot. You'll find baked goods such as *fatayer* (pastry pockets filled with spinach, meat or cheese) and sizzling hotpots (try the cheese, ham and egg combo), but ZwZ, as it is known, is most famous for its *manakeesh*, often referred to as Lebanese pizza. The description is accurate in that *mankoushe* (the singular) is a flat-baked bread with toppings, but it comes in both savoury and sweet varieties and can be ordered as *furn* (a thick base) or *saj* (lighter and crispier). Try the *zaatar w jebneh saj* (thyme and cheese) or a *lahme beajine* (minced meat and tomato), and finish up with a *chocolat w moze saj* (banana and chocolate). Absolute heaven.

Sheikh Zayed Road, near the Shangri-La Hotel, T 339 8310

11.00 Al Ahmadiya

Until the 1950s, Dubai was a big village split into three areas: Deira, Shindagha and Bastakiya. These have been swallowed up by expansion, but Deira's Al Ras district remains a superb place to see what Dubai looked like before it discovered oil. It's a mishmash of old and new, decaying low-rises, a few towers, and beautiful coral-stone-and-gypsum merchant houses. Al Ahmadiya, Dubai's first school, was built by a pearl trader in 1912, and current ruler Sheikh Mohammad was educated here. This two-storey building has reed ceilings, decorative archways and plaques with Koranic verses. The school shut in 1963 but was saved from ruin in 2000; it and the trader's house behind are now museums. Note that on Fridays it opens at 3pm. *Al Khor Street, T 226 0286, www.dubaitourism.ae/cultureheritage*

15.00 Mojo Gallery
Over the last decade, the industrial quarter of Al Quoz has attracted an influx of galleries. Spend an afternoon here to glimpse what's motivating young artists from Beirut to Bombay. A highlight is Mojo, which is dedicated to promoting contemporary international and regional art in all its forms.
Unit 33, Al Serkal Avenue, Street 8, T 347 7388, www.themojogallery.com

18.00 Pierchic

Perched at the end of a pier, this dark, fortress-like place with its curious little wind towers looks rather gothic. The walkway can seem endless, but once you arrive, the laidback bar and magnificent view of the sea and Burj Al Arab (see p013) make up for the exertion, especially after a cracking Kir Royale. Pierchic is also a restaurant and, as befits its location, the menu is mostly seafood. Prices are steep, especially since the portions tend towards the *nouvelle*, though the quality of ingredients is evident in every bite. However, the real pleasures to be had here are of the liquid kind. So order a cocktail, settle down on one of the sofa loungers on the deck and wait for one of Dubai's stunning sunsets.
Madinat Jumeirah, T 366 6730, www.jumeirah.com

URBAN LIFE
CAFÉS, RESTAURANTS, BARS AND NIGHTCLUBS

Nightlife in Dubai can be rather too much like nightlife in Europe, the US or India. Clubs host DJs who were in Goa the night before and are on their way back to Barcelona, while comedy clubs feature acts fresh from London. The biggest immediate difference, apart from the abundance of Arabian-themed interiors, is that strict control on alcohol means that bars, clubs and good restaurants (of which there are many, often run by award-winning chefs) are in five-star hotels. An escape from the lobby scene is the seaside vibe at Sho Cho (Dubai Marine Beach Resort & Spa, Jumeirah Beach Road, T 346 1111). If you aren't fussed about drinking, sample the gourmet delights at The Jumeirah Garden Guesthouse (see p016), courtesy of chef Andy Campbell.

For something raw, visit the eateries of Deira and Karama. Most don't serve alcohol and so attract a non-Western crowd. You'll find everything from Italian to Tibetan cuisine. Feast on cheap-as-chips Punjabi dishes at Ravi Restaurant (Al Satwa Road, T 331 5353) or eat Iraqi food at Al Beit Al Baghdadi (Al Muteena Street, T 273 7064). Decent local cuisine is scarce outside private homes, so if you want some *dango* or *ouzi*, you'll have to hit the tourist traps. Try Local House (65 Bastakiya, next to Majlis Gallery, T 354 0705) or the dancing-camels-with-buffet blowout at Al Hadheerah (Jumeirah Bab Al Shams Desert Resort & Spa, T 809 6287). *For full addresses, see Resources.*

The Edge

Applying the maxim that if you have to look at a price tag you probably can't afford it, The Edge's cheapest option is its 400-dirham business lunch. The restaurant would also much rather that you let the chef make the decisions for you. Set menus are available, but for those who can surrender control, Yerson Behi's food is a fantastic culinary experience. The menu changes daily (stalwart ingredients include Wagyu beef, foie gras and Hokkaido scallops), but the cooking is consistently impressive without ever feeling the need to rely on scientific trickery or coronary-inducing sauces. The refreshingly austere surroundings are by Munich-based firm Flint Skallen. A reservation is essential. *Gate Precinct, Building 6, DIFC, T 363 7770, www.theedge.ae*

Caramel Restaurant & Lounge
Given the comparisons made between
Dubai and Las Vegas, it's only fitting
the connection has been made concrete.
In 2010, the people behind the Caramel
Restaurant at the Bellagio opened a
branch here, drawing the crowds with
sophisticated American fare, a roomy
terrace and glamazon hostesses.
*Level 2, Gate Village, Building 3,
DIFC, T425 6677*

Rhodes Mezzanine

Brit chef Gary Rhodes opened Mezzanine in 2007, and it was immediately seen as a rival to arch-nemesis Gordon Ramsay's Verre (T 212 7550). Although it is the more casual of the two, Rhodes' restaurant has proved the more successful. The loyal crowd at this Studitalia-designed venue come to sample an untraditional take on quintessentially British dishes such as pork belly, squab and crab, as well as schoolboy desserts like spotted dick. In less-capable hands (Paul Lupton runs the kitchen on Rhodes' behalf), these sweets would be marathons of stodge. But here they are transformed into delicate concoctions of sugar and spice. Guaranteed, despite the adult décor, to bring out your inner child.
Grosvenor House, T 317 6000,
www.grosvenorhouse-dubai.com

The Lime Tree Café

It will probably remind you a little of the wholefood cafés you used to eat in as a student, but The Lime Tree has several appealing features. First, it offers one of the rare opportunities in the city to eat good food outside a hotel or a shopping mall. Second, it serves excellent, if simple, dishes. And third, your body will thank you for giving it a break from all the spices, seafood and steak you've been feeding it of late. Huge but interesting salads, pies, quiches, frittatas and mountainous desserts are best washed down with a lime and mint cooler. The lavish breakfasts are popular with the baby-on-board crowd and the place is usually packed with newspaper-toting expats, but don't let that deter you. It's a colourful treat.

Jumeirah Beach Road, T 349 8498,
www.thelimetreecafe.com

Reflets

Stylistically somewhere between a boudoir and a brasserie (or even a bordello – the bathrooms are nothing short of dramatic), French chef Pierre Gagnaire's restaurant is a winner. The dishes are exquisitely presented works of art, interpreted here by Olivier Bile, and the emphasis is on all things fresh or, rather, freshly flown in; with the exception of locally caught fish, the ingredients come from elsewhere. The cuisine is characterised by the kind of taste and texture combinations best described as 'multisensory hits', and hints at molecular cuisine without ever straying into its more rarefied expressions. As it's hoped diners will sample a number of courses, portions are designed to titilate not to sate. *Intercontinental Festival City, T 701 1111, www.ichotelsgroup.com/intercontinental*

The One Deli

Located in a store that's a cross between Pier 1 and The Conran Shop, this dramatic café, with its glass-bead curtains and Louis Farouk furniture, is popular, you won't be surprised to discover, with male interior decorators and their female friends. The One is about as close as Dubai gets to a gay café, and the menu is fabulous too, featuring healthy, mix'n'match deli-style dishes, sandwiches and cakes, unusual fruit juice combinations, including a watermelon-and-chilli cooler, and more varieties of tea than you thought could exist. Survey the clientele, who are possibly surveying you, or just enjoy the view of the imposing neo-Fatimid-style Jumeirah Mosque next door.
Jumeirah Beach Road, T 345 6687, www.theoneplanet.com

Almaz by Momo

Mourad Mazouz's Middle Eastern outpost is a riot of *zellije* tiles, intriguing stencil designs, dark-glitter ceiling panels and brightly coloured terrazzo tiles from Lebanon. The menu is light and flavoursome modern North African and the attractive, multicultural staff will be more than happy to advise. Eat in the main room (above), choose the more secluded confines of the tent-like dining area or savour a selection of snacks as you smoke a water pipe in the Shisha Lounge. Almaz is alcohol-free but some of the mocktails are so convincing, you may just get a buzz anyway.
3rd Floor, Harvey Nichols, Mall of the Emirates, T 409 8877, www.altayer.com

Rare Restaurant

Dubai isn't short of places in which to sink your teeth into a piece of meat. There's The Exchange Grill (T 311 8559), the Belgian Beer Café (T 701 2267) and even Argentine churrasco at La Parrilla (T 406 8999). The city isn't short of places serving up Wagyu treats either, though not usually as steak. This is not the case at Rare, which is all about the flesh. The menu does include some appetising alternatives to meat – lobster pancakes or guinea fowl, for example – but when you can choose some of the finest cuts of Kobe or Angus beef in town, accompanied by a faint hint of beech from the wood grill, you probably won't bother.

Desert Palm Resort, Al Awir Road, T 323 8888, desertpalm.peraquum.com

The Roof Top

Yes, the view is a little less attractive now that The Palm occupies half the horizon, but the atmosphere at The Roof Top remains as seductive as ever. Hypnotic music, a mixture of lounge and chilled-out Middle Eastern, and the low, cushion-covered divans combine to create a lethally serene atmosphere. So you might as well play pasha for a day. Slip off your shoes, sink into the cushions, order a cocktail and a couple of plates of mezze, and forget the world exists. Though not necessarily the right place for making new friends – the crowd is beautiful but cliquey – this is an intimate venue to visit with the one you love or want to know better.
Arabian Court, One&Only Royal Mirage, Al Sufouh Road, T 399 9999, www.oneandonlyresorts.com

Okku

Don't let Okku's beautiful crowd of media darlings, Eastern European models, Gucci-clad domestic celebutants and see-and-be-seensters put you off. Most of them make for the private dining areas upstairs, which are reminiscent of the tatami rooms at kaiseki-ryori restaurants in Japan. And do not allow the DJ booth, the jellyfish tanks or the pulsing fibre-optic wall that separates the bar and dining area to mislead you into thinking that Okku is anything other than a restaurant, because the food is marvellous. Only the sushi and sashimi are strictly Japanese, but signature dishes such as yellowfin tuna carpaccio in a ponzu dipping sauce will tempt the strictest of purists.
The Monarch Hotel, 1 Sheikh Zayed Road, T 501 8777, www.okkudubai.com

Indego

Though you will eat in the company of Hindu gods and South Asian tchotchkes, the interior at Indego, by local firm LW Design Group, is sufficiently specific to say 'India' but sufficiently uncluttered to leave your focus squarely on the food. This is as it should be for, much as he does at his Michelin-starred Rasoi in London, Vineet Bhatia continues to offer Dubai diners some of the most interesting contemporary Indian cuisine in town. The menu is a mixture of traditional dishes with a twist and out-and-out fusion – prawns poached in coconut milk with chilli masala, for example – and is both daring and delicious.

Grosvenor House, West Marina Beach, T 317 6000, www.grosvenorhouse-dubai.com

Left Bank

Nibbles and late breakfasts are served at the weekend, but eating at Left Bank is besides the point. This is a bar, pure and simple, popular for its wide selection of moderately priced wines and some of the finest cocktails in town. There are two branches in Dubai. The one at the Madinat Jumeirah (above), with its large terrace, is popular with the city's younger Western expats. Its newer, more sophisticated sister (T 368 4501), tucked into a corner of Downtown's Souk Al Bahar, attracts a slightly older, less rambunctious crowd. Both are flirty, but the lower volume of music at Souk Al Bahar means that, in a city where public displays of affection can land you in jail, being able to talk makes it easier to deal with any sudden impulses. *Madinat Jumeirah, Al Sufouh Road, T 368 6171, www.emiratesleisureretail.com*

Zuma
This outpost of the Japanese franchise
occupies a sprawling, double-height
space in the DIFC – an inspired location,
given the prices. Choose between the
sushi counter, the more formal dining
area or relax in the low-lit upstairs
lounge (pictured), complete with
a beautiful antique-wood sake bar.
*Gate Village 6, Trade Centre 2, DIFC,
T 425 5660, www.zumarestaurant.com*

Neos
Some places are less about what they
are than where they are. While it would
be inaccurate to suggest that the
chrome-heavy cocktail bar Neos falls
into this category, its lofty position at
the top of The Address Downtown (see
p024) is a major part of its appeal. The
seating is arranged to maximise the view.
*Emaar Boulevard, T 436 8927,
www.theaddress.com*

INSIDER'S GUIDE

NADINE KNOTZER, GALLERIST

Born and raised in Vienna, and of Iranian and Austrian parentage, Nadine Knotzer moved to Dubai in 2008 with her partner, Kourosh Nouri, to launch what has become one of the city's most interesting galleries, Carbon 12 (Warehouse D37, Street 8, Al Serkal Avenue, Al Quoz 1, T 050 464 4392). The duo's fresh take on contemporary art and knack for discovering talent has turned their gallery into a local fixture. For an afternoon break, Knotzer favours Shelter brasserie (Warehouse 209, 318 Road, Al Quoz 4, T 434 5655), and when she isn't working, she can be found perusing the aisles of Harvey Nichols (Mall of the Emirates, T 409 8888). She also often pays a visit to Essa (S*uce, Shop 29, The Village Mall, Jumeirah Beach Road, T 050 634 6524), a UAE-Indian fashion designer based in Sharjah known for his use of vintage fabrics and bright colours.

For a taste of home, Knotzer loves Persia Persia (Wafi, Oud Metha, T 324 4100) for its modern interior, *koobideh* kebabs and the chance to enjoy a fruit-scented water pipe on the terrace (from August to April). For something funkier, she drops in to Smiling BKK (Al Wasl Road, next to Jumeirah Post Office, T 349 6677), which, despite its oddly named dishes (Day Tripping Buddha, for example) and kitsch décor, is all about home-style Thai cooking. After dark, she mingles with the media crowd on the beanbags by the pool at Shades (The Address Dubai Marina, T 436 7777). *For full addresses, see Resources.*

ARCHITOUR

A GUIDE TO DUBAI'S ICONIC BUILDINGS

Billy Idol once said that he was an idol because he called himself one. Dubai has apparently taken a leaf from the singer's book and labours under the belief that by labelling every new building 'iconic', however undeservedly, the description will stick. Even up to a decade ago, the Gulf hadn't progressed much beyond its coral-stone-and-adobe vernacular, so if you threw up a tall building you could claim the cutting edge. That is no longer the case. Inspired by Dubai's success, and flush thanks to an oil boom, Abu Dhabi, Qatar, Bahrain and Kuwait appear to have decided that their future cachet should, in part, be based on starchitecture.

Although the financial crisis spelled the end for most of Dubai's more outré projects, including Dynamic Architecture's Rotating Tower, put others on hold (Zaha Hadid's Signature Towers and Opera House) and slowed down the remainder, such as Lord Foster's The Index (312 Road, DIFC), it may also have had a more positive effect. The city's fall from financial grace appears to have chastened it, and it could be more inclined to embrace quality over quantity. The fact that Rem Koolhaas' mega Waterfront City has not been cancelled suggests that this may be the case. If not, in about a decade or so, when its neighbours come into their own, Dubai's star will wane. If there were anything the city that hype built could not bear, it would be to surrender the limelight to its sisters.

For full addresses, see Resources.

Burj Khalifa

From its wide base, this Y-shaped tower, designed by SOM with Adrian Smith, spirals upwards, sections falling away, until in the last few hundred metres the slender central core emerges. Opened in January 2010, the world's tallest building is a mixed-use tower – the Armani Hotel (see p017) occupies 12 of its floors – which soars 828m into Dubai's dusty sky. Its shape is based on the geometry of a desert flower, but the impression of Gotham on Viagra is too powerful to miss. Islamic architectural motifs are also alluded to, albeit in a largely symbolic manner, and technical tricks include a double-glass skin and a lift that makes its way to the observation deck on the 124th floor in 60 seconds.

1 Emaar Boulevard, T 888 8124,
www.burjkhalifa.ae

The Gate

Yes, you have seen something similar before – in Paris. Got it yet? No? Well then picture a cartouche of romantic neoclassical sculpture on either column, replace the square arch with a round one and you could almost be on the Champs-Élysées. The gateway to Dubai's new business hub shows that tasteful reinterpretation is no bad thing.
DIFC, Sheikh Zayed Road, www.difc.ae

National Bank of Dubai

This 1998 bank building is the work of Uruguayan Carlos Ott, the architect of the reviled L'Opéra Bastille in Paris, and was arguably Dubai's first deliberately iconic building. It is certainly Ott's best work, at least in Dubai. His much-lauded Hilton Dubai Creek revamp is cold in comparison, and his B2B Tower in Business Bay is also uninspiring. But this 124m-tall tower, with its sail-shaped glass façade, is meant to evoke the dhows that ply the Creek, and the tension in the arc of its mirrored surface suggests the building is about to sail across the city. It is especially attractive just before dusk, when it catches the light of the setting sun and sends it shimmering across the water; and after dark, when the lights from the offices within turn it into a giant electronic display.
Baniyas Road, T 310 0101

O-14 Building

Wedged between much taller towers, Business Bay's striking O-14 Building is already overlooked, but if the images on the billboards advertising the 200-odd other towers planned for the development are any indication, it is never likely to be overshadowed. In a city enamoured of reflective-glass cladding – a practice that requires industrial-strength air-con to offset the heat of the Gulf – O-14 presents a solidly concrete face. Admittedly, it is riddled with 1,326 holes, and in this, New York-based Reiser + Umemoto's design is reminiscent of Toyo Ito's Emmental-esque Mikimoto boutique in Ginza. But in O-14, the holes are unglazed and the 40 to 60cm-thick shell acts as a sunscreen. Also, it is 1m from the glazing, trapping a layer of colder air to help cool the building. *Sector A05, Business Bay*

Dubai Creek Golf & Yacht Club

This club is not only the city's most conveniently located golf course, smack in the middle of town between the business district of Garhoud and the Creek itself, but its clubhouse is also one of Dubai's most distinctive buildings. It opened in 1993, designed by UK firm Godwin Austen Johnson, known for championing a modern Arabian style at hotels such as the One&Only and Bab Al Shams. The sharply curving planes that lock above the glass atrium are pure futurism, and pay homage to the simple sailing boats that once dominated the Creek. The clubhouse has the feel of a Middle Eastern take on the Sydney Opera House, but most visitors probably don't notice, attracted instead by an 18-hole par-71 championship-standard course, and a floodlit nine-hole course that can be played until 10pm.
Al Garhoud Road, T 295 6000, www.dubaigolf.com

SHOPPING

THE BEST RETAIL THERAPY AND WHAT TO BUY

Consumerism is a national sport in Dubai, and when temperatures regularly exceed 40°C, who'd want to be kicking a football around anyway? The sheer number of brands, all tax-free, explains the appeal to visitors from India, Iran and the neighbouring states. For most others, there's not a lot on offer. In a city where everything comes from somewhere else, there isn't much that your average Londoner, Singaporean or Tokyoite couldn't find at home.

But it isn't all bad. The souks are fun and, while they don't have the cachet of the malls and lack the gravitas of the souks in Aleppo in Syria and Shiraz in Iran, they are atmospheric places to wander around. Dubai is short on boutiques and small businesses, but it is still a young city. Art galleries such as The Third Line (Al Quoz 3, T 341 1367) and Gallery Isabelle van den Eynde (Al Quoz 1, T 323 5052) are creating a regional hub, and designers are slowly arriving. Try Soirée (Villa 11, Al Wasl Road, between interchange 1 and 2, T 349 4995) for Pakistani fashion and Western designs.

What Dubai does offer is custom-made goods. Bring a photo of what you want, find material at the Textiles Souk (off Al Fahidi Street) and haggle hard at tailors such as Kachins (Cosmos Lane, Meena Bazaar, T 352 1386) or Dream Girl (Al Fahidi Street, T 352 6463). For jewellery, try the Gold Souk (Old Baladiya Street) or upscale Gold & Diamond Park (Sheikh Zayed Road, T 347 7788). *For full addresses, see Resources.*

O' de Rose

This Jumeirah concept store is a wonderland of domestic delights, cool knick-knacks, artwork and women's fashion. The collection is envisaged as a showcase for Middle Eastern and central Asian goods, and embraces both the contemporary and the traditional. Standout pieces include midcentury furniture reupholstered in embroidered antique fabrics, future-antique brassware and the modern tables inlaid with mother-of-pearl. There are also Syrian mirrors and an impressive selection of Iranian, Turkish and Moroccan porcelain to keep the more traditionally minded home decorator in orientalist heaven. *999 Al Wasl Road, Umm Suqeim 2, T 348 7990, www.o-derose.com*

Katrin Greiling

Commissioned to develop contemporary furniture inspired by and made in Dubai, Swedish industrial designer Katrin Greiling chose not to follow the usual route of Islamic geometries and ironic references to tradition. Instead, she focused on this once-nomadic nation's inability to settle into sedentariness. The resulting 'Bidoun' (Arabic for without) collection includes sofas with or without backs – such as this one (above), 12,500 dirhams – constructed from upholstered slabs lashed together with cord; and a coffee table with rope handles. All the pieces are solid-looking yet portable. The line can be found at Dubai's most impeccably curated furniture store, Traffic (T 341 8494).
www.katringreiling.com

Villa Moda

You may wonder if the DIFC's twin Villa Modas (there's a his and a hers) are midcentury furniture or high-end clothes stores, and to keep you guessing both are for sale. It's a clever concept. Opened but no longer run by Kuwait's Sheik Majed Al-Sabah, this is still the best shop in town for the forwardly fashionable. *Gate Village, DIFC, T 382 5160 (women), T 382 5150 (men), www.villa-moda.com*

Boom & Mellow

If the chandeliers, faux antiques and purses hanging off the walls don't already make it clear that Boom & Mellow is all about the girls, the glittering jewels in the glass cases will. This boutique has a little bit of everything from everywhere, which sets it apart from the monocultural sterility of most of Dubai's outlets, and it's a great place to get a sense of what's going on in Egypt, Lebanon, Syria and, to a lesser degree, Dubai. Best buys include the vibrant purses by Sarah's Bag and luscious jewellery by Shourouk, such as this necklace (above), 4,390 dirhams.
Shop F47, 1st floor, Mall of the Emirates, Sheikh Zayed Road, T 341 3993, www.boomandmellow.com

Shiffa

When Dr Lamees Hamdan couldn't find any anti-stretchmark oil she trusted when she was carrying her first child, she decided to make her own. Of course, as a trained dermatologist, Hamdan did have an advantage, but the range she created, which includes bath oils, skin creams and aromatic candles, is the work of someone who is passionate about taking care of much more than just the surface. Organic, preservative-free and hypo-allergenic, the luxurious, richly scented products, which are sold under the Shiffa brand (the word means healing in Arabic), are made from ingredients sourced across Africa and Asia. Available in Harvey Nichols (T 269 0887) in the Mall of the Emirates.
www.shiffa.com

SPORTS AND SPAS
WORK OUT, CHILL OUT OR JUST WATCH

Doha may well have pipped Dubai to the post by creating a national sport academy (ASPIRE) to train the Qatari athletes of the future, but Dubai is no quitter, and hopes are high that it will recover at least some lost ground once the long-awaited and even longer delayed US$1.9bn Sports City development is finally completed in 2011. Parts of it, including a world-class cricket stadium (T 425 1111, www.dubaisportscity.ae), are already open, but the crucial training academies are yet to see the light.

When it comes to armchair sport, though, Dubai still has the market covered. In the winter, when temperatures are more palatable, one international event follows another. Apart from homegrown pleasures such as weekly camel racing, highlights include the World Power Boat Championship, the Dubai Rugby Sevens in December, the Dubai Tennis Championship, the Desert Classic golf event in February, and the world's highest-stakes horseracing event, the Dubai World Cup (see p084), in March.

The more active can take fitness classes at the Metropolitan Hotel (Sheikh Zayed Road, T 343 0000), pick up a bow and arrow at the Dubai Archers Club (Sharjah Wanderers Golf Club, T 050 588 0951), go scuba-diving with Al Boom Diving (Al Wasl Road, T 342 2993) or Scubatec (Shop 15, Karama Sana Building, T 334 8988) and tackle the 400m downhill run at the indoor Ski Dubai (see p086). *For full addresses, see Resources.*

Amara

A treatment session at the Amara spa
in the Park Hyatt (see p022) is a serious
business. Start with a foot and hand wash,
followed by a Dead Sea Salt Bath (45
minutes, 160 dirhams), then rinse off in
the outdoor rain shower in your private
courtyard. Relax in the garden with some
tea, dried apricots and almonds before
returning for an aromatherapy treatment
(1 hour, 420 dirhams) or Swedish massage
session (1 hour, 420 dirhams), where you
will be alternately pounded and slathered
with oils that leave your skin soft for days.
Return to the shower, then move to the
central courtyard where, in the evening,
the oil lights in the pool and the star-filled
sky will relieve any residual tension. Leave
remade and ready to fall into bed.
*Park Hyatt, Al Garhoud Road, T 602 1234,
www.dubai.park.hyatt.com*

Spa at The Address Downtown

Dubai isn't short of five-star spas, most of them staffed by nimble-fingered South-East Asians trained to massage even the most recalcitrant muscles into blissful acquiescence. The Address' two-hour signature treatments, Restore and Rejuvenate, place you in the perfect state to luxuriate in the post-treatment panoramic views of the Burj Khalifa (see p065), Dubai Mall and the faux crenellations of Old Town. But the real reason to come here is the hotel's five-tiered pool, to which spa-goers have access. It never feels crowded and is built in such a way that sinking to eye level in the lowest pool leaves you with only the Dubai Fountain and the base of the world's tallest tower for company. *Emaar Boulevard, T 436 8888, www.theaddress.com*

Meydan Racecourse

It goes without saying that the Dubai government's 60,000-seat racetrack is the largest in the world. Less expected were the 12 non-stop hours of live local TV coverage it enjoyed when it opened in early 2010. Still, it's an impressive beast, equipped with both turf and Tapeta tracks. The equestrian season is capped by the Dubai World Cup, the race with the highest prize purse in the world. Meydan's ambitions don't end there. It's also home to a five-star hotel and a slew of fine-dining restaurants, and when the development is complete, facilities will include an IMAX cinema, a golf course, a marina, a museum, stables, a residential quarter and, of course, plenty of shops.
Al Meydan Road, Nad Al Sheba,
T 327 0000, www.meydan.ae

Ski Dubai

A trip to Dubai, the self-styled Las Vegas of the Middle East, would not be complete without indulging in at least one tacky experience. So remind yourself that you are in one of the most surreal cities in the world and head for the five indoor slopes at Ski Dubai. Late evenings are probably best for avoiding first-timers (open until 11pm, Sun-Wed; midnight, Thurs-Sat).
Mall of the Emirates, Sheikh Zayed Road, T 409 4000, www.skidxb.com

ESCAPES

WHERE TO GO IF YOU WANT TO LEAVE TOWN

So much conspicuous consumption eventually wearies even the most ardent capitalist. When thoughts turn to escape, Dubai offers four options: the desert, the sea, another emirate or a flight out. The last is the sole option for a genuine change of scenery. As for neighbouring cities, it's only in terms of development and amenities that the six other emirates differ. That said, a trip to Sharjah (see p100), Ras Al Khaimah (see p102) or the capital Abu Dhabi (see p092), which has development plans that make Dubai look like a test run, will give a better sense of regional context.

Alternatives include Kish, Iran's kooky, veil-optional island of relative decadence, the stunningly beautiful 16th-century mud-brick towers of Shibam and Sana'a in Yemen, and a weekend trip to visit the museums and other contemporary architectural additions to Bahrain's historic Al Muharraq neighbourhood, which is fast becoming the Gulf's most interesting arts quarter.

In winter, the desert has myriad attractions. There are historic forts (Al Bithnah), ancient villages (Hatta), archaeological sites (Wadi Al Hayl), hot springs at Ain Al Ghamour (rough and ready, not Zumthor) and dune-bashing (www.desertsafaridubai.com). A note, though. Unless you're a connoisseur of kitsch, pass on any packages that combine an afternoon of adrenaline with visits to Bedouin 'encampments', henna tattoo sessions or belly dancing. *For full addresses, see Resources.*

Museum of Islamic Art, Doha

Doha isn't short on stunning modern architecture – it's just that nearly all of it is located on the Qatar Foundation campus and casual visits are not possible. Luckily, IM Pei's blockily beautiful Museum of Islamic Art, opened in 2008, single-handedly makes the visit to Doha worthwhile. Rising 60m off the seaside corniche, this austere white meditation on geometric shapes – a dome that becomes an octagon that becomes squares that become triangles – is undeniably of today but is replete with references to the past. Jean-Michel Wilmotte's minimalist interiors (above) provide the showcase for one of the world's best collections of Islamic art forms, from calligraphy to ceramics. There are daily flights from Dubai with Emirates and Fly Dubai.
Al Corniche, T 00 974 422 4444

Abu Dhabi

The largest of the seven emirates that make up the UAE, Abu Dhabi is not only the country's capital and centre of political power, it is also its richest city, floating on a sea of oil that resource-strapped Dubai can only envy. Smaller and less glitzy than its more famous sister, Abu Dhabi retains traces of the modest fishing port it was when oil was first discovered in 1958, but not for long. The city is positioning itself as the region's cultural epicentre, with better-funded arts festivals and a slew of new mega-museums. Rising on Saadiyat Island are Frank Gehry's Guggenheim and Jean Nouvel's Louvre. Elsewhere, the state's bold ambitions are visible in the form of cutting-edge buildings like the 499-room Yas Hotel (pool, above; T 02 656 0000), which straddles a Formula 1 racetrack and the sea in Yas Marina.

Liwa Oasis

Arrive in Dubai expecting *The English Patient*-style vistas and you may feel let down. The desert is indeed vast, and while around Dubai it's pretty enough, with rippling dunes and, further out, views of jagged mountains, it rarely feels remote. At first glance, the oasis town of Liwa, 150km south-west of Abu Dhabi, might not seem so either, but drive out of town and you'll find yourself on the eastern fringes of the Empty Quarter, a vast sea of sand that stretches across the Arabian Peninsula. From here to the mountains of Taif on the Saudi Arabia-Yemen border, there's nothing but dunes. Camp if you wish or stay at Anantara's Arabian-themed Qasr Al Sarab Desert Resort (pictured; T 02 886 2088) for some five-star pampering coupled with uninterrupted views.

Isfahan, Iran

An hour's flight from Dubai (Iran Air flies twice a week), Isfahan is Iran's equivalent of Rome or Athens. The beloved city of the Safavid emperors and twice the capital of Persia, it feels like a vast, open-air museum. It's hard to know where to start. How about Naghsh-e Jahan square – so large it's nicknamed Nesf-e Jahan or 'half of the world' – which is flanked by the frescoed 17th-century Ali Qapu Palace and the Sheikh Lotfallah Mosque, with its breathtaking mosaic dome? Or the stunning Imam Mosque (opposite), or 11th-century Friday Mosque (above)? Or the restored Ali Gholi Agha Alley bathhouse, the Hasht Behesht palace or Armenian churches of Vank? Perhaps something older? If so, the ancient capital of Persepolis and rock-cut tombs of Naqsh-e Rustam are an hour up the road.

Six Senses Hideaway Zighy Bay, Oman
A leisurely drive from Dubai through a series of progressively sleepy desert towns and, ultimately, over the starkly serrated mountainscape of Musandam (until recently a lawless land of pirates and smugglers), the Six Senses Zighy Bay makes a virtue of isolation. Built along traditional Omani lines, the neat buildings, with their stone-and-mud walls, wooden beams and low, cube-like forms, are screened by strategically planted palms and woven lattices. But if the feel is rustic, the service is anything but. Whatever you wish to do in the 'Arabian fjords' – be it hiking, snorkelling, dolphin-spotting, deep-sea fishing or swimming from cove to deserted cove – Six Senses will oblige.
Musandam Peninsula,
T 00 968 2673 5555, www.sixsenses.com

Sharjah

The emirate of Sharjah doesn't look a bit like its bigger sister. Admittedly, your first sight is of a shopping mall, but soon you'll notice the high-rises aren't as high, the hotels aren't as many-starred and the restaurants are more sober. There is an emphasis on Islamic values (no alcohol, nightclubs, short sleeves or miniskirts), Arabic dominates, and in place of glitzy malls there are museums and 'traditional' bazaars. Family values, prohibition...you may be wondering why on earth you would visit? Although Sharjah may be too sedate to live in, it is home to the majority of the museums in the UAE. Those devoted to archaeology (T 06 566 5466), Islamic civilisation (T 06 565 5455) and art (T 06 568 8222) are all of interest. If you must shop, head for the Blue Souk (Corniche Street, near Khaled Lagoon).

Banyan Tree Al Wadi, Ras Al Khaimah

Set amid the sand dunes and the ghaf trees of a private nature reserve in the Wadi Khadeja, the Banyan Tree's first Middle Eastern property blends Asian styling and Islamic motifs to create a contemporary Arabian aesthetic. Eschewing faux historicism and overblown Bedouinisms, the resort is a combination of tents and villas, laid out in a way that maximises views without sacrificing privacy. Many of the individual pools, for example, are shielded from one another by dunes. With a signature restaurant overlooking a watering hole and a series of watchtowers strewn across the 100-hectare site, guests are assured that, should their fellow lodgers fail to interest them, there's plenty more wildlife to observe.
Al Mazraa, T 07 206 7777,
www.banyantree.com